PUERTO RICO:
AMERICA'S 51ST STATE?

PUERTO RICO:
AMERICA'S 51ST STATE?

by David J. Abodaher

AN IMPACT BOOK
FRANKLIN WATTS
NEW YORK/CHICAGO/LONDON/TORONTO/SYDNEY

Photographs copyright ©: North Wind Picture Archives, Alfred, ME: p. 1; The Bettmann Archive: pp. 2, 5 top; New York Public Library, Picture Collection: p. 3; Hunter College, Center for Puerto Rican Studies: pp. 4, 5 bottom; AP/Wide World Photos: pp. 6 top, 10, 12, 14, 16; UPI/Bettmann Newsphotos: pp. 6 bottom, 7, 9, 11, 15; Culver Pictures, Inc.: p. 8; National Baseball Library, Cooperstown, N.Y.: p. 13.

Library of Congress Cataloging-in-Publication Data

Abodaher, David J.
Puerto Rico: America's 51st state? / by David J. Abodaher.
p. cm.—(An Impact book)
Includes bibliographical references and index.
Summary: Surveys the history of the island nation of Puerto Rico, from its colonization by Spain through its time under American control to debate over statehood and independence.
ISBN 0-531-13024-X
1. Puerto Rico—History—Juvenile literature. 2. Statehood (American politics)—Juvenile literature. 3. Self-determination. National—Puerto Rico—Juvenile literature. [1. Puerto Rico—History.] I. Title.
F1958.3.A26 1993
972.95—dc20   92-39474 CIP AC

CONTENTS

☆
To Dr. Alfred Habeeb
with thanks for fifty years of friendship
and for his beautiful Carmen

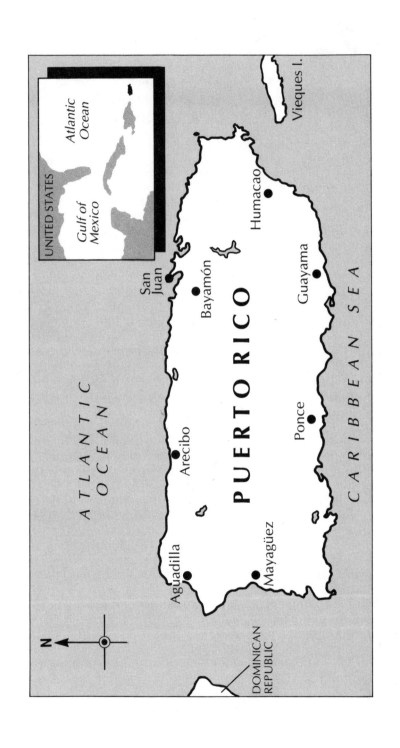

1
AN
OVERVIEW

Puerto Rico is one of more than 7,000 islands in the huge archipelago (cluster of islands) known as the West Indies. The name West Indies stems from the fact that it is the area stumbled upon by European explorers trying to reach India and the Orient by sailing west.

The multitude of islands that make up the West Indies includes the Bahamas, which are located off the southeast coast of Florida. Positioned almost directly east of Miami, the Bahamas consist of hundreds of islands of which only thirty are inhabited. Once a British Crown Colony, the Bahamas are now an independent nation.

South of the Bahamas are the Greater and Lesser Antilles, stretching through the Caribbean Sea as far as the northern coast of South America.

The most significant of the islands known as the Lesser Antilles are Barbados, Trinidad, and Tobago.

The four major islands that compose the Greater Antilles are Cuba, Jamaica, Hispaniola, and Puerto Rico. Hispaniola includes both Haiti and the Dominican Republic.

No other island group in the world matches the West Indies in the number of islands or extent of territory. The archipelago stretches more than 1,500 miles (2415 km) from the southeast coast of the United States to the South American continent, and west to east some 500 miles from the coast of Venezuela to Puerto Rico.

At one time—a very long time ago—the entire West Indies complex of islands did not actually exist. Historians and geologists tell us that more than 100 million years ago the entire region which now comprises Puerto Rico on the east to the American continents on the west was covered by the waters of the Atlantic Ocean. Eventually, still countless centuries ago, massive earthquakes burst through the Atlantic waters, and islands like Puerto Rico, as well as the continents of Central and South America were created. West of Puerto Rico, an inland sea, later called the Caribbean, came into being.

Archaeologists and geologists have been unable to pinpoint the exact time when Puerto Rico became inhabited by humans. However, they have determined that centuries ago an ancient people, referred to as the Archaics, made their way into the Caribbean from the mainland of what is now Florida or Georgia. Using huge floating rafts, the Archaics arrived first at Cuba, then other islands, finally coming to Puerto Rico. Historians know very little of the Archaics' years in the Caribbean islands.

The next group to invade Puerto Rico was the Igneris from the Orinoco River region of Venezuela. Arriving in huge canoelike boats, these people

☆ **10** ☆

brought the first evidences of any civilized skills. They were expert fishermen, and also were highly accomplished in the creation of pottery and vibrantly colored ceramics.

The Igneris were followed by another group from the Arawak culture, the Tainos. From what is known of them, it seems that the Tainos were a more knowledgable and sophisticated group than those who preceded them. They were the first people to give their island home a name. They called what is now Puerto Rico *Boriquen*—Land of the Regal Lord.

The Tainos in Puerto Rico established a structured society by developing villages throughout the island. Although the villages were small, they were all laid out according to a single plan. Each contained an open area in the center, resembling the town square of many American towns. This open area was called the *batey*. From each side of the square, narrow lanes stretching toward the village limits were lined with rudely constructed living quarters.

The batey was the focal point for all the social activities of the Tainos, such as town meetings and religious ceremonies. Tribal dances were also held there. So, too, were games. One game played by young boys of the village somewhat resembled soccer.

The Tainos' social structure was much like that of the Incas of South America. Each village settlement had a leader who acted much as a mayor does in today's society. Also, the island as a whole had a leader who was elected from among the village chiefs.

The structure of Taino society was based on a *caste* system that was simpler than that of the Incas. The top level included the island chieftain and his family and the village chiefs and their families. At the second level of power were the medicine-men priests of each settlement.

The combined responsibilities of health and spiritual guidance made the medicine man the most respected and needed individual in each Taino settlement. He cured various ailments with a number of herbal teas, looked after the people's emotional needs, and warded off evil by chanting prayers to the god of good to protect the Tainos. In order to appease the god of evil, who might bring damaging storms and earthquakes to the island, he sniffed finely ground tobacco. This would put him into a deep trance, bringing him in contact with the god he needed.

The simplified caste system divided the Tainos' general population into two groups. The largest group was made up of a huge laboring force. The other group, which was answerable to the chieftain and medicine man, was a service, teaching, and supervisory unit. This group instructed the laborers in tilling the soil for growing a wide variety of vegetables and herbs that were the mainstay of the Taino diet.

The Taino economy was predominately agricultural. The people grew sweet potatoes, corn, peppers, peanuts, and cabbage. Also, the laborers gathered fruits and cotton, which grew wild throughout the island. In some unknown manner, they wove the cotton into undyed cloth that was used to make garments. In general, the laboring Taino was a hardworking citizen.

By the middle of the fifteenth century, there were more than 25,000 Tainos living on Boriquen. Throughout the years they withstood raid after raid as other tribes attempted invasions and takeovers.

In time, however, they were assaulted by a South American people, the Caribs, whom they could not totally conquer.

The Caribs, after whom the area and the sea were named, roamed the nearby waters in huge boats. Time and again they raided Taino villages, taking women and children back to their homes in South America. When the Europeans arrived at Boriquen Island late in the fifteenth century, the Taino population was all but decimated.

During the next four centuries, Spain looked upon the island as one of its more important colonial territories, one which brought it considerable wealth.

Puerto Rico's location at the eastern extremity of the Greater Antilles made it a target for attack by other nations, but all were repelled. Puerto Rico continued through the four hundred years to be the most stable of the many islands in the Caribbean. Unlike Cuba and Haiti, where attempts were made to shake off Spanish control by riots and turmoil, Puerto Rico remained loyal to the Spanish throne. There were, nonetheless, a number of movements toward independence.

In 1898 a Cuban revolt brought on the Spanish-American War. The ultimate United States victory made Puerto Rico an American possession. Then, after fifty or so years of rule by Washington, the island was granted status as a semi-independent commonwealth of the United States. Puerto Rico was then able to govern itself and elect its own leaders.

Feeling secure under American protection, one large segment of the Puerto Rican population started a campaign for stronger ties with the American mainland. Hawaii had not yet become America's fiftieth state when Puerto Ricans began to push for statehood.

This fervent hope for statehood was not shared by all Puerto Ricans. A second group demanded total independence. Puerto Rico, they declared, should be a free republic. A third group clamored to maintain the status quo; let Puerto Rico retain its position as a commonwealth, governing itself but answering to the president and Congress of the United States.

The reasons for these diverse choices will be discussed later. As we have already entered the last decade of the twentieth century, the three-way battle rages on.

2
BORIQUEN
BECOMES
PUERTO RICO

In 1485, King Ferdinand and Queen Isabella of Spain granted an audience to Christopher Columbus, a navigator from Genoa, Italy. They were intrigued by his claim that he could reach India and the Orient by sailing due west across the Atlantic Ocean. It would be, Columbus told the royal couple, a much shorter and less hazardous trip than the usual route around the Cape of Good Hope at the southernmost tip of Africa.

Ferdinand and Isabella agreed to fund Columbus's voyage in 1492 and on August 3 he sailed from Spain with three ships—the *Nina*, the *Pinta* and the *Santa Maria*. On the morning of October 12, 1492, he landed at an island that is part of the group now called the Bahama Islands. Columbus named the island San Salvador.

Leaving San Salvador, Columbus sailed south to explore other islands in the Caribbean. At each stop, sailors were sent ashore to gather vegetables, fruits, and plants. On these expeditions, the Spaniards also discovered gold.

The Caribbean island now known as Hispaniola was the last stop on the famous trip of 1492; here, one of the three ships was wrecked. Columbus then sailed back to Spain with his gold, artifacts, and a number of natives whom he felt certain were Orientals. Because of their copper-colored skin, and his belief that he had found India, he called his captive natives Indians.

The king and queen of Spain were extremely pleased with Columbus's report, and with the gold and artifacts that he had brought back. Of course, they did not know that it was not India that Columbus had found, but, rather, the beginning of a Spanish colonial empire. With visions of great wealth, thanks to the gold nuggets and new Spanish territories, the royal couple sent Columbus on a second voyage.

However, the course Columbus took on this second voyage was somewhat farther south than the previous one. On the morning of November 19, 1493, Columbus and his fleet of seventeen ships landed at an island called Boriquen by its native Tainos. When Columbus set foot on the island he claimed it for Spain, as he had done previously with San Salvador and Hispaniola. In honor of Saint John the Baptist and Juan, the son of King Ferdinand and Queen Isabella, he named the island San Juan Bautista.

This new discovery of Columbus's was not a huge island. It was about half the size of Hispaniola and the smallest of the Greater Antilles, covering less than 3,500 square miles. Shaped like an uneven rectangle, it stretched only 110 miles (177 km) east to west, and just under 40 miles (64 km) north to south.

When Columbus came ashore, no natives were seen. Frightened by the sight of so many large ships, and men carrying weapons and wearing colorful uniforms, the Tainos fled to the island's interior.

Walking along the golden sandy beaches facing the Atlantic Ocean, Columbus turned inland from the shore and found a small village located on a long, narrow inlet. He was struck by the beauty of a bay fringed by tall trees. He named the village Puerto Rico, which in Spanish means rich or beautiful port.

Soon some of the more daring Tainos came out of hiding. Through gestures, Columbus made contact and was able to learn of their amazing accomplishments. He was impressed by the pottery they showed him, and even more so by the bright pieces of stone which he immediately perceived to be gold. Columbus took many of these trophies back to Spain. It is estimated that there were more than 30,000 Tainos on the island when Columbus left.

Back in Madrid, Columbus enthusiastically reported to King Ferdinand and Queen Isabella about all the surprising wonders he had found. He told of how the Tainos, with only simple, handmade tools, had built a series of beautiful communities. He described the villagers' homes as "artfully made, although of straw and wood; and there was a plaza, with a road leading to the sea, very clean and straight, made like a street. . . . and beautiful gardens, as if they were vineyards or orchards of citron trees such as those in Valencia or Barcelona. . . ."[1]

Before leaving for Spain Columbus had commanded a garrison of Spanish officers to maintain order in the new colony. Once Columbus was gone, the Spanish officers lost little time in brutally perse-cuting and torturing the Tainos.

Soldiers, with guns pointed, pushed Tainos into the Atlantic waters to gather fish and forced them to walk the shore in search of crabs and other shellfish. With threatening guns in hand, the soldiers coerced the natives to dig for gold. Those who hesitated were thrashed. Any who rebelled were shot.

The helpless Tainos began to fight back, but they were no match for the armed Spaniards. Under the darkness of night, small groups found boats and escaped to other islands. In the early years of the sixteenth century, there were only about 4,000 Tainos left in Puerto Rico.

In 1508, another Spanish explorer, Juan Ponce de Leon, established the first genuine town on the island, naming it Caparra. The arrival of Ponce de Leon marked the beginning of the end for the Taino culture in Puerto Rico. Skirmishes between the na-tives and the Spaniards erupted almost immediately after Ponce de Leon landed with a force of more than a hundred Spanish soldiers. Altercations con-tinued for three years.

Soon after Ponce de Leon sent the ship which he had sailed on back to Spain, the Tainos began a series of assaults on Caparra. Led by the chieftain of a village near the newly named settlement, the na-tives made nightly raids against the Spaniards.

To counter these attacks, Ponce de Leon led a troop of 125 men into the mountains north of Ca-parra where the Tainos were entrenched. Hiding behind trees in small gulleys, the Spaniards opened fire on a force of some hundred Tainos. The assault was a short one, for a randomly fired bullet killed the Taino's chief.

With the Spanish forces watching and holding

their fire, the Tainos picked up their fallen chief and retreated. The death of their leader had shattered the fighting spirit of the people. The Tainos became demoralized. Never again would they be an effective and fearless fighting force. The Spanish colony prevailed.

Ponce de Leon offered the Tainos amnesty if they would work in the mines and fields. They would have none of it. Many left in canoes under the shield of darkness, determined to find another island that they could call home. Others destroyed their children, so that they would not grow up to become slaves of the enemy; still others committed suicide.

As gruesome and tragic as the desperate actions of the Tainos were, they did bring about some measure of quiet to the island. So few Tainos remained that Ponce de Leon had a serious problem: there was a dire need for help in gathering the gold nuggets that sparkled in the river beds. Ponce de Leon solved the labor problem by bringing African slaves from Spain. The slaves also worked the tobacco and sugar cane fields, and picked the cotton that flourished wildly throughout the island.

Then, unfortunately for him, Juan Ponce de Leon became the victim of political intrigue. He believed himself to be the governor of the island by virtue of appointment of the king. In 1511, however, the right to name the ruler of any island in the Caribbean controlled by Spain would be carried out by the governor of Hispaniola. In effect, this governor supervised all the islands under Spanish control. The Hispaniola governor rejected Ponce de Leon's claim and named a friend, Juan Ceron, to the post. Embittered by this, Juan Ponce de Leon sailed away to look for the Fountain of Youth, eventually discovering Florida.

☆ **19** ☆

The king and queen of Spain wasted no time in solidifying their hold on Puerto Rico. They dispatched Dominican priests to the island to ensure its existence as a Roman Catholic entity. Also, rules and regulations for trading were established. Unfortunately, Spain often neglected to provide essential needs for the colony, thus hindering its progress. In 1511, the island's present identity was formalized. The village on the bay named Puerto Rico by Columbus became San Juan, the island's capital. The island itself ceased to be known as San Juan and became known as Puerto Rico.

By the middle of the sixteenth century, Columbus's fortunate mistake had brought Spain colonies that covered almost half of the Western Hemisphere. Included were Florida, Mexico, all the countries in what is now Central America, and eight countries in South America ranging from Venezuela in the north to Chile at the southern tip. Of course, there were Puerto Rico, Cuba, Hispaniola, and other islands in the Antilles.

One of Puerto Rico's most serious problems during the early years of Spanish occupation was the stabilization of an island economy. Ponce de Leon's discovery of gold did little for the long term. Gold there was, but no gold mines, only gold nuggets on the many riverbeds, there for the taking. And they were taken for a short time, first by the early settlers, then by the Tainos, and later by the African slaves.

As a result of the preoccupation with gold, all other resources on the island were overlooked. Only after the surface gold in the rivers was gone was it decided to consider agriculture as a means for keeping Puerto Rico afloat. The tobacco and cotton that grew freely and wildly throughout most of the 3,465 square miles were the first exports from Puerto Rico to foreign lands. Then, sugar became the most important commodity, one that proved to be a welcome import to Spain, to other colonies, both of Spain and of other European countries.

In the year 1523, Puerto Rico's first sugar mill was built in the village of San German near the southwestern tip of the island. It marked the beginning of a Puerto Rican economy that would have its "ups and downs" throughout the centuries ahead. The sixteenth century, in particular, was one of unending turmoil. The Spanish settlers were forced to fight off one serious problem after another.

For one thing, despite having controlled the Tainos' raids to a great degree, the Spaniards still lived in constant fear of invasion. The warlike Caribs who had scattered through a few other islands constantly besieged the Puerto Rican mainland. In 1528 they burned down the village of San German. Among other Carib raids was one on October 18, 1529. On that day three boatloads of Caribs entered the bay of San Juan and attempted to carry off a number of Spaniards and African slaves. In this attack, a number of Caribs were killed by the Spaniards with a shot from a cannon that was on shore. During another Carib raid in October 1530, near the village of Cristobal de Guzman, a plantation was destroyed.

An even more formidable threat of invasion faced Puerto Rico during the last half of the sixteenth century and beyond. Spain's European neighbors were jealous of Spain's extensive colonization of the New World. Determined to get their share of the wealth in gold and precious stones, the French, Dutch, and English began assaults on Spanish ships and the Spanish colonies in the West Indies.

Again and again, Spanish ships sailing to and

☆ **21** ☆

from the New World were fired upon from the high seas. The English, French, and Dutch attacked Spanish colonies, including Puerto Rico. All three European countries were intrigued by Puerto Rico's strategic location at the eastern edge of an area containing countless desirable islands. And because of that location, Puerto Rico was an important military stronghold.

The invaders were turned back by Puerto Rico, but they did manage to colonize some of the other islands in the area. Great Britain conquered islands to the north, including the site of Columbus's first discovery of San Salvador. What is now known as Bermuda was another English conquest. The French and Dutch took over a number of smaller islands in the Lesser Antilles.

To help thwart further invasions, Spain sent Puerto Rico material to build stronger fortifications. Forts at San Juan and other strategic ports exist today as colorful and interesting tourist attractions.

Periodic attempts to invade Puerto Rico continued. In 1595, England's Sir Francis Drake made a futile attempt to conquer the country. The Earl of Cumberland was also driven off in 1598.

Nature itself vented its wrath on Puerto Rico. Heavy tropical storms whipped up by strong westward winds from Africa often assaulted the islanders. Occasionally, hurricanes brought devastation. In a single year during the 1530s, three such hurricanes swept over the island.

Health hazards were commonplace during those early years. Disease was rampant because there were few hospitals and doctors. Many severe epidemics cost hundreds of lives. Finally, Spain helped to ease the problems by providing the money to build more hospitals and to supply more doctors.

By the end of the sixteenth century, the social development of Puerto Rico was well under way. Two distinct classes of islanders emerged: Those who lived in San Juan and in the villages along the Atlantic and Caribbean coasts, and those who lived inland and in the mountain regions.

Residents in San Juan and other coastal towns had the best of it. The townspeople had churches, hospitals, and markets. Their houses, which were hardly pretentious, provided some measure of protection from the elements. The town settlers were, however, restricted to a degree in their daily lives by the government rules and regulations.

The settlers who lived inland and in the mountains chose a simpler way of life. Freedom from governmental restrictions provided them with the ability to live as they pleased, and to them was worth any inconvenience they might suffer. These islanders chose to live off the land and use leaky thatched huts for homes.

At the end of the sixteenth century, Puerto Rico was on its way to becoming the strong and viable land that Spain had wished it to be. However, a near disastrous attack remained to be foiled. The Dutch, in 1625, made one last attempt to invade Puerto Rico.

Since Spain was at war with the Netherlands, the Dutch decided to bring Spain to its knees by making a last ditch effort to take away that country's most prized colony. On a September morning in 1625, with 2,500 soldiers aboard seventeen ships, the Dutch attempted a landing at San Juan.

A long, violent, and bloody battle ensued between the Dutch force of 2,500 and the small 325-man contingent of islanders led by Governor Juan de Haro. The Dutch burned San Juan to the ground,

☆ **23** ☆

but could not penetrate or bombard El Morro, the largest fortress overlooking the harbor. Frustrated by the impenetrable walls of El Morro, the Dutch invaders returned to their ships and sailed away.

Saved once again, the islanders turned toward rebuilding San Juan, their capital city.

3
A
NEW WORLD
TAKES SHAPE

During the seventeenth century, the face of the globe changed radically. When tiny Puerto Rico proved itself a David in driving off the Goliaths of Europe, the British, French, and Dutch were forced to look elsewhere for lands to colonize.

For almost two centuries, the giants of Europe had ignored opportunities to lay claim to lands in the New World. Blinded by the glitter of gold, they bypassed the northern reaches of the Americas until they realized that the areas south of Florida were closed to them.

Great Britain could have led the way.

In the year 1497, an adventurous man named John Cabot sailed across the Atlantic and landed in Cape Breton Island. After claiming all of this new-found world for Great Britain, he returned home and excitedly spoke of the great schools of fish that were there for the taking. He was not only ignored, he was laughed at.

But this was not so in France, which soon learned of Cabot's discovery. Fishermen along France's Brittany coast were determined to get their share of Nova Scotia's edible riches. One explorer named Jacques Cartier discovered the Gulf of St. Lawrence in 1534, and then the St. Lawrence River. He became convinced that the river was the fabled Northwest Passage to China and the Orient.

In the early 1600s, Samuel de Champlain also searched in vain for the Northwest Passage. However, Champlain also had the vision to see this new land as a strong and profitable colony for his country. Not until the hunters for beaver fur arrived, such as Pierre Radisson and Daniel Duluth, did the French government pay any serious attention to the possibilities in the Americas. In 1672 the French government sent Louis de Frontenac to govern its new possession, the colony of New France. This opened the way to further exploration of the North American continent. Joliet and Marquette discovered the upper reaches of the Mississippi River. LaSalle followed, exploring the rest of that great river to its mouth, and claiming the Louisiana Territory for France.

The Dutch were the next to lay serious claim to any part of North America. After their last defeat at the hands of the Puerto Ricans in 1625, the Dutch fleet sailed north and took possession of what is now New York, which they called New Netherlands, and founded a settlement named New Amsterdam at the mouth of the Hudson River.

Great Britain was actually last to colonize in the New World, despite the fact that Pilgrims fleeing religious persecution in England landed in 1620 at

Plymouth Rock in what is now Massachusetts. Later, of course, the British not only possessed the North Atlantic seaboard but also expelled the Dutch from New York and the French from Canada.

Meanwhile, Puerto Rico busied itself with repairing the great damage caused by the Dutch. Money and materials came from the Spanish royal family to rebuild San Juan and to further strengthen Puerto Rican fortifications. It was a slow and difficult job, interrupted often by repeated invasions. While the European assaults had diminished, the warring Carib tribes still vented their wrath against Spanish domination of the area.

A major problem in trying to restore San Juan was the shortage of laborers. Black slaves had deserted the cities and hidden themselves in the mountains. In 1664, the governor, Juan Perez de Guzman, found the answer. He decreed that all Africans who would swear allegiance to Spain and be baptized into the Catholic religion would be given their freedom. As word spread, Africans from other islands in the Caribbean flocked to Puerto Rico.

The eighteenth century, like the one before, is remembered in history as ten decades of conflicts and wars, resulting in a series of changes in the map of the Western Hemisphere. This time, however, it was the northern section of the Americas that changed and not the southern.

During the early years of the eighteenth century, Great Britain solidified its hold on the thirteen colonies along the east coast of North America. Florida alone remained under Spanish control. In 1759, on Quebec's Plains of Abraham, the British defeated the French and took over all French possessions, except Louisiana. (Louisiana was bought by the United States from the French in 1803.)

In the American colonies, militant Massachusetts colonists protested an English tea tax, dumping tons of tea into Boston harbor in 1773. The American Revolution (1775–1783) led to the eviction of Great Britain, and the emergence of the United States of America.

The creation of the thirteen American states was a boost to the Puerto Rican economy. Trade began to develop between Puerto Rico and the new nation. Puerto Rico sent sugar, coffee, molasses, and tobacco to America. The United States sold flour, wheat, and other essentials to Puerto Rico. During a five-year period, as the eighteenth century came to a close, United States ships entered San Juan harbor more than twenty-five times.

Even though conditions were improving in Puerto Rico, the island found itself warding off British invasions. In 1797 Great Britain was at war with Spain. On April 17 of that year, having just taken over the island of Trinidad from Spain, two British forces, one army and one navy, made an assault on Puerto Rico. As the British troops began moving toward San Juan, they were surprised every few minutes by hidden Puerto Rican militia. Such skirmishes continued for two weeks, and the British foot soldiers never reached San Juan. Finally, the British retreated and left Puerto Rico, having accomplished nothing. The British tried invading again in December 1797, in 1799, in 1800, and in 1801, all resulting in similar failures. When the Treaty of Amiens ended the war between England and Spain, the British erased Puerto Rico from their colonizing plans in the Americas.

During the three hundred years since Columbus had claimed Puerto Rico for Spain, the island was regarded more as a fortress protecting the entrance to the Caribbean and other Spanish island colonies than as a territory providing riches and products useful in the mother country. From the beginning, this shortsighted approach on the part of Spain had held back economic development of Puerto Rico. Through most of the three hundred years, Puerto Rico was limited to trading only with Spain itself. Trade with other Caribbean islands, Mexico, or the many Spanish colonies in South America was prohibited.

Opportunity knocked when Spain became involved in its war with the British. Though there was some limited trade with other Caribbean colonies and with the United States, it did increase in the early years of the nineteenth century. Puerto Ricans, including government officials, began smuggling products into and out of the island, even though all trade was against Spanish regulations.

With new markets, agriculture, the backbone of the Puerto Rican economy, began to flourish. This, in turn, meant a need for more laborers. In a short time, Puerto Rico's population swelled from less than 50,000 to more than 155,000.

Most of the new settlers came from Spain and the Spanish-controlled Canary Islands, located off the northwest edge of Africa. Some came from nearby Caribbean islands such as French-controlled Haiti, and from Louisiana's heavy French population. Others landed from Florida, which had been sold in 1819 to the United States.

This great influx of immigrants was the direct result of a decree issued by the king of Spain. It promised a grant of land to any person who would come to Puerto Rico and swear loyalty to the king and adopt the Catholic religion. This decree saved Puerto Rico and its newly awakened economy. As

☆ **29** ☆

trade blossomed with other Caribbean territories and with the new United States of America, Puerto Rico became an economic asset for Spain.

The many plantations scattered throughout the island had been ignored by the Spanish government for too long. The sugarcane and tobacco fields, the fruit orchards, and the sugar mills needed more workers to bring about maximum production for the newly expanded export opportunities. The new decree brought those needed laborers, but still more were needed, as well as more modern tools and equipment. Even in the nineteenth century, laborers were still using medieval and archaic means to till the soil, plant crops, and reap the harvests. Hand-pushed plows, crudely constructed of wood with an iron tip, were frequently broken. The only other tools available were axes, hoes, and crudely fashioned machetes. Little or no investment had ever been made in more up-to-date machinery and other equipment.

Another facet of the governmental decree helped to ease this problem to some extent. It provided for the free and unrestricted importation of farm equipment. Also, it freed cash for equipment purchases by removing the tax on slaves owned by the plantation owners and supervisors. Puerto Rico was finally appreciated for the pesos it could pour into the Spanish treasury. The island's economic growth had at last been stabilized.

Despite the passage of centuries, the Puerto Rican social structure had changed only a little. The population, now nearing a million, was still divided into two classes: the haves and the have-nots, whether they lived in city areas or in the rural sections. The majority of Puerto Ricans lived in rural

☆ **30** ☆

areas away from the coast. There were only thirty-four cities or villages. Most were on one of the four seacoasts.

The wide disparity in population between cities and rural areas made it difficult for the government, based in San Juan, to govern the entire island. Fewer than 15 percent of the people lived in the cities and villages, with more than 85 percent of the inhabitants scattered throughout the mountains and other inland regions. To complicate matters, communication between cities and inland communities was nearly impossible. There was only one decently surfaced road between San Juan on the Atlantic coast and Ponce on the Caribbean, almost directly south. Other connections, whether between coastal cities or between inland villages, were dirt roads that became totally impassable during the frequent rainstorms.

One might well imagine the hardships suffered by the more than 60 percent of Puerto Ricans living in the outlying areas who were engaged in agriculture as a way of life. Once the sugar and tobacco crops barely produced enough for daily needs; now the increased trade made them a profitable business. Yet little was being done to improve living conditions and communications within the rural areas. It was not because of any lack of interest on the part of the government; officials were preoccupied with what seemed to them more important.

In 1809 Governor Toribo Montes was mostly concerned with what was happening in Spain itself. A Spanish warship arrived in San Juan harbor bringing news that France had invaded Spain. Napoleon Bonaparte had, without warning, stormed into Madrid. Not only had he seized the Royal Palace, he had also kidnapped King Ferdinand VII and taken him as prisoner to France. In Ferdinand's place, Napoleon installed his brother, Joseph Bonaparte, as king of Spain. Although Spanish resistance to this situation had already driven Joseph Bonaparte back to France and the legitimate Spanish monarchy was already restored, Governor Montes was unaware of these events and busied himself with protecting Puerto Rico against a possible takeover by France.

Ironically, Puerto Rico and other Spanish colonies in the Americas benefited from Napoleon's short-lived aggression. To protect itself against other similar problems and make its colonies an integral part of the Spanish empire, a Supreme Council was established. Based in Madrid, it would include representatives from each of the Spanish colonies including Puerto Rico. Each representative could then plead for his own colony's needs.

Although this new organization did bind Puerto Rico more closely to the empire, it had the opposite effect on most other colonies. One by one, each began to fight for total independence from Spain. The breakaways began early in the nineteenth century as many colonies in South America rebelled.

First to declare independence from Spain was Venezuela, in 1811. Led by Francisco de Miranda and Simon Bolivar, Venezuelan patriots finally overthrew the Spanish government in 1821. One by one, all the Spanish colonies in South America declared their own independence and became sovereign states.

Near the end of the century, the island colonies, except for Puerto Rico, made their bids for separation from Spain. There were occasional vocal, but not armed, uprisings in Puerto Rico calling for independence; however, none was successful. The Spanish government became concerned and called

☆ **32** ☆

on Puerto Rico to send its representative to the Supreme Council as soon as possible.

Nearing the end of his term, Governor Toribo Montes decided not to appoint a representative. The new Puerto Rican governor, Salvador Menendez, went one step further. He brought a touch of democracy to the island by deciding that the representative should be chosen in an open election. The voting took place in Puerto Rico's five principal cities: San Juan, San German, Coamo, Arecibo, and Aguada. The man who was elected, Ramon Power Giral, was one of the most respected leaders in Puerto Rico.

At the time of his election, Giral, who was born in San Juan in 1775, was in Santo Domingo, leading a contingent of Puerto Rican and Spanish soldiers to quell a rebellion demanding independence from Spain. Loyal to Spain, intelligent, and somewhat liberal-minded, Giral was considered the ideal person to represent the island.

Called back to San Juan, he discussed Puerto Rico's needs with Governor Menendez. Of prime consideration were issues of trade, education, and the building of roads for better communication between areas on the island. All three issues were vitally important not only to the economic progress of Puerto Rico but also to the welfare of each individual resident.

Trade with the outside world is the lifeblood of any community. Puerto Rico had products that would be welcome in nations throughout the world. There was coffee, sugar, fruits, vegetables, and livestock. For too long, the Spanish government had restricted trade only with Spain and only using Spanish ships.

Some Puerto Rican products reached other markets because some plantations smuggled them to

☆ **33** ☆

the United States and Europe. A few people became immensely wealthy by violating Spanish laws.

Ramon Giral's presence in Madrid as Puerto Rico's representative finally opened the trade doors. The entire island began to reap the benefits. San Juan had suffered most because of trade restrictions. While the smugglers traded Puerto Rican products for tools, machinery, clothing, and other goods, the average Puerto Rican in San Juan starved for lack of food.

Education throughout the island was another serious problem that Giral was able to address. The Spanish government agreed to establish an improved educational system for its colony, and to provide for the construction of schools and the building of highways to make schools more accessible for those who lived in remote areas. A much needed change was finally in the works.

Far too many Puerto Ricans had reached adulthood unable to read or write. Illiteracy was a prime problem in Puerto Rico even after more than three centuries of Spanish control. Government officials had closed their eyes to the need for a literate society. There were few schools, generally confined to the five or six largest urban areas. Even those were mostly church schools with attendance dependent on the ability to pay tuition. No schooling was available to either children or adults in the inland and mountain areas.

Most of the blame for the indifference to educational needs in Puerto Rico belonged to the government in Spain. Within the royal hierarchy, there had been the belief that education would encourage Puerto Rican leaders who would lead movements of independence from Spain. Ramon Giral was able to change Spanish thinking on the subject. Slowly but inevitably, Spain gave more money for education.

Slow as it was, there was some progress. Spain sent architects, construction experts, and even well-trained teachers. A comparatively small annual budget produced primary and secondary schools, books, and other needed materials. Within forty years, some 300,000 children were enrolled in Puerto Rican schools. The illiteracy rate dropped from a bit over 90 percent to just over 30 percent. After this had been accomplished, a commissioner of education was appointed, leading to a system which covered the primary grades through graduate school.

Despite the promise of better things to come, the last half of the nineteenth century was a period of upheaval for both Spain and Puerto Rico. In Spain, the monarchy had been driven from power twice and replaced with a stricter military authority. Twice the king returned to power. For whoever was in charge, the great concern was holding on to the remaining colonial possessions. One by one, all of Spain's colonies except Puerto Rico and Cuba had become independent. And keeping those two became more difficult.

In both Cuba and Puerto Rico, an undercurrent of desire for independence was growing. Cuban cries had often turned violent, but in Puerto Rico there was little or no open expression of violence in a try for independence until the 1860s. During this decade, a doctor in San Juan, Ramon Emeteria Betances, began to call openly for an armed revolt against Spain.

Betances had been exiled several times, but after each absence from the island he returned more defiant. In 1867 Betances was exiled again, this time

☆ 35 ☆

to Spain. He escaped and made his way to New York, a city to which many hundreds of Cubans and Puerto Ricans had migrated in search of employment. In New York, Dr. Betances recruited Puerto Ricans and others of Spanish background, preaching revolution, independence from Spain, and an end to Spanish oppression. Satisfied that the time was ripe for rebellion, he returned to Puerto Rico.

Dr. Betances settled in the mountainous region of west central Puerto Rico near the village of Lares. Nearby was a coffee plantation owned by a Venezuelan named Manual Rojas, who had lived in Puerto Rico since he was a boy and who shared Betances' passion for independence. His hacienda became headquarters for the secret underground militia that he and Betances put together.

During early planning sessions at Rojas's farm, Betances designed a flag similar to the American Stars and Stripes. The centerpiece of the design was a wide white cross. Two of the corners were red and two were white. In the center was a single white star.

On September 23, 1868, some 500 revolutionaries moved out of the Rojas plantation armed with guns, rifles, and machetes. They entered the village of Lares and set up a provisional government, proclaiming Puerto Rico an independent nation. Their next plan was to take over the city of San Sebastian.

The attack on San Sebastian was a failure. The revolutionaries were met by a Spanish force made up of army soldiers and militia. Four rebels were killed and seven taken prisoner. Rojas and many others were sentenced to death (but later pardoned), while Betances managed to escape to France.

Beginning in 1895, a series of historic events led to a *radoca*—a change in Puerto Rico's future. Early in that year, Cuban nationalists were again embroiled in a bloody fight with Spanish troops. Cuba was determined to achieve independence, whatever the cost. As word of Spanish persecution against Cubans reached the United States, a great wave of sympathy for the Cubans swept across the country.

In a gesture of friendliness and support, the United States government sent the battleship *Maine*. It was intended to be no more than a friendly visit, but on February 15, 1898, the ship was sunk in Havana harbor. What caused the sinking or who was responsible has never been determined. The American public, however, rose in anger and the cry "Remember the Maine" became a familiar anti-Spanish slogan.

Spain called a truce with the Cubans on April 8. For a moment, it seemed the issue was settled and Cuba would become an independent, self-governing state. The United States immediately backed Cuba, issuing a formal statement that Cuba must be free.

Then, on April 24, 1898, Spain declared war on the United States. The following day, President William McKinley responded with a declaration of war against Spain. The Americans waged the short war on two fronts: in the Caribbean sector and in the Pacific with an assault on the Spanish-held Philippine Islands. Two men gained great fame in this dual campaign. One was Theodore Roosevelt, who led his First Volunteer Cavalry, known as the Rough Riders, in the Battle of San Juan Hill. The other was Commodore George Dewey whose squadron won the Battle of Manila in the Philippines.

The Spanish-American War ended on July 17, 1898, with American victories on both fronts. Almost as an afterthought, American troops landed in

Puerto Rico. From one end of the island to the other, confidence that Puerto Rico would now gain independence swept over the land. For many, it was to be a hope unfulfilled.

Involved discussions took place between American and Spanish representatives as they met to determine the terms of peace in the Treaty of Paris, which was signed on December 10, 1898. In the end, the United States was awarded the Philippines, Guam, and Puerto Rico.

4

THE AMERICANIZATION OF PUERTO RICO

Hope grew in the hearts of many Puerto Ricans as the Americans took possession of the island. Their confidence increased as knowledgeable people spoke of recent happenings in the western areas of the United States. The case was made that Wyoming had been a territory much like Puerto Rico before becoming the forty-fourth state in 1890; and, Utah, which was taken over after the Mexican War, had also been a territorial possession before being admitted as the forty-fifth state in 1896. Was it not probable that Puerto Rico would follow the same pattern?

Others were not so hopeful. They could not believe that Puerto Rico would be better off under American domination than it had been under Spanish rule. Also, they were fearful that their Spanish culture and traditions would soon fade away. Still others demanded complete independence with the argument that Puerto Ricans alone should determine the fate of Puerto Rico.

Puerto Rico was ruled by the United States War Department during the first two years of American control, a fact not appreciated by its entire population. A modified civil government came into power in 1900 when the United States Congress passed the Foraker Act, which treated Puerto Rico as a stepchild. The Foraker Act gave no consideration to the Puerto Ricans' needs or desires. The Puerto Rican government which was organized under the Foraker Act was almost a mirror image of the federal government as set up by the United States Constitution. There was an executive, legislative, and judiciary branch of government.

The executive branch was headed by a governor appointed by the president of the United States with the approval of Congress. The governor, like the American president, had a cabinet of officials also appointed by the president. The other two branches were similarly set up. A two-house legislature made laws and regulations. However, members of one group were appointed by the American president. The other legislative branch, called the Council of Delegates, gave Puerto Ricans their only voice as to their needs and wishes. The delegates were elected by Puerto Rican citizens. But the council's authority was limited to debates and making recommendations. As another sop to Puerto Rican pride, an elected delegate could represent the island in Washington and sit as a member of the House of Representatives. However, like the members of the Council of Delegates, he could only make speeches and recommendations on behalf of his country.

The person elected as Puerto Rico's representative in Washington was Luis Muñoz Rivera. A scholar, writer, poet, and an astute politician, his is one of the most famous names in Puerto Rican history. His son, Luis Muñoz Marín, would later emerge as an even more distinguished leader in Puerto Rico's history. (To avoid confusion over the slight difference in the names of father and son— Spanish custom calls for the use of both the father's surname and the mother's maiden name—the father's name is after the baptismal name and then the mother's maiden name; that is, baptismal name, Luis; father's surname, Muñoz; mother's maiden name, Marín.)

Whatever help Puerto Rico received during the early years of American possession was due to the efforts of Luis Muñoz Rivera. Few members of the United States House of Representatives knew about Puerto Rico nor did they care to learn. Only after hearing Rivera's articulate and persuasive speeches did they react to the needs of the new colony. Funds for the construction or repair of schools, hospitals, roads, and bridges were approved.

In 1917, Congress passed the Jones Act, which gave Puerto Ricans American citizenship. It also allowed Puerto Ricans to elect members to both houses of the island legislature. The Jones Act gave Puerto Ricans a little more say in governing themselves. And with war rumblings in Europe and World War I in the wings for America, the Jones Act also made all young Puerto Rican men eligible for the U.S. military draft.

Whether too busy with other matters, or merely disinterested, the American Congress paid no attention to Puerto Rico's economy. Never very stable, the economy had gone from bad to worse. While the islanders were still under Spanish control, the peasants and plantation owners had lived off the

☆ 41 ☆

profits from coffee, sugar, molasses, and rum. Now there was not enough to feed the mushrooming population. When the United States took over Puerto Rico, its population was less than 950,000. By 1922, it had ballooned to 1,350,000 with no slowdown in sight.

There was hope for better things to come when American businesses started moving into Puerto Rico. However, it was a vain hope. Since modern technology made many operations unnecessary, jobs were still at a premium. In the thirty years after the American takeover of Puerto Rico, exports rose from $8 million to $100 million. American businessmen profited immensely from the sugar and coffee exports.

But the tremendous profit earned by the American enterprises did little to help Puerto Rico. Most of the profits went back to the American mainland. The rest was used in building new plants and modernizing old ones. To make matters worse, the American ventures were eating up too much Puerto Rican land. Ignoring a law passed by Congress which stated that no one could own or lease more than 500 acres, some American businesses were buying parcels of 30,000 to 500,000 acres. No one was ever prosecuted for these greedy violations.

As Puerto Rican land was eaten up by big business, the small landowner suffered. American land purchases forced small landowners to leave the soil that had supported their families. In a short time, more than 60 percent of all Puerto Rican laborers were without jobs, with nothing being done to ease their plight. The more than a dozen governors appointed by Washington did nothing. None spoke Spanish or understood the Spanish culture. Each merely put in his time enjoying the days in the tropical sun.

Not until 1929, when Theodore Roosevelt, Jr., was appointed governor of Puerto Rico, did any official concern himself with Puerto Rico's needs. Serious-minded and dedicated to his assignment, the young Theodore Roosevelt was soon aware of the hopeless conditions which faced the islanders. He toured the island, going from city to city and into the mountain regions, and saw firsthand the deplorable conditions. He made regular reports of his findings to the United States Congress.

Unfortunately, little or nothing was done. After the stock market crash of 1929, the United States itself was in economic turmoil. It wasn't until 1933, when President Franklin Delano Roosevelt initiated his New Deal, that some measure of relief came to Puerto Rico.

Roosevelt's New Deal created many governmental agencies that spent vast amounts of money to assist the needy and the underprivileged. It also developed programs that provided work for the unemployed. Puerto Rico benefited from Roosevelt's initiative. Two programs were especially created to fill Puerto Rico's needs, both short-term and long-term.

One program was planned to meet the urgent and immediate needs of the hungry. It provided government-subsidized jobs that permitted the most helpless to earn enough money to at least feed themselves. The second program, somewhat related, was called the Puerto Rico Reconstruction Administration. It also addressed the means of increasing employment, since it brought about the construction of public housing, modernization of old buildings, clearance of slum areas, and the building of small factories. In addition, it helped to develop farm cooperatives and hydroelectric facilities. Another important benefit was the training of young scientists to research Puerto Rican problems, determine solutions, and implement them. Many of these young men later became leaders in movements to improve Puerto Rico's industrial and social structure.

The emergence of intellectuals, thinkers, writers, poets, and professors brought widespread debate about Puerto Rico's future. Organizations and political parties began to declare loudly, sometimes with violence, their perceptions of Puerto Rico's tomorrow. From the earliest years of Puerto Rico's role as an American satellite, various factions clamored for one of three ways to go.

One would cry out that Puerto Rico could best survive under American supervision. A second would claim that Puerto Rico deserved to be a state of the United States. A third group would declare that total independence as a sovereign nation was best for the island. The champion of this third group was none other than Luis Muñoz Rivera, who had the good sense not to antagonize the American Congress by declaring his views openly. Nonetheless, he continued to work quietly toward that end. His views and his work for the improvement of the island were continued by his son, Luis Muñoz Marín.

Luis Muñoz Marín was born in San Juan in 1898, just before the American takeover. His youth and school years, from high school through college, were spent in Washington, D.C., while his father served as Puerto Rico's delegate to the House of Representatives. Attending prestigious Georgetown

University, it is not surprising that Marín understood American ways and American thinking.

After his father's death, he wanted no more of Washington, but he did not move back to Puerto Rico. Instead, newly married, Muñoz Marín settled in New York City, where he devoted himself to writing poetry and magazine articles and translating English poetry into Spanish. He was as fluent in English as he was in Spanish. Soon he became bored with his life in New York and began to miss his native Puerto Rico.

Upon his return to San Juan, his Spanish heritage took hold. Perhaps because he felt deeply the fact that his father had died before seeing his hopes of a free Puerto Rico materialize, or perhaps also because politics was deeply ingrained in his heart and mind, Muñoz began to do what he could to make his father's dream come true. Not long after his return to Puerto Rico, Luis Muñoz Marín joined the Liberal Party, which had been established by his father. He also took over publication of his father's newspaper, *La Democratica*. His editorials constantly promoted independence as Puerto Rico's only way to survive.

By 1932, Muñoz was as thoroughly immersed in Puerto Rican politics as his father had been. He made a successful bid for election to the Puerto Rican Senate, where he became more acutely aware of the unemployed and the extent of their hunger and poverty. Independence for Puerto Rico was no longer his primary concern. He determined that other, more important things needed to be taken care of.

Muñoz began to implement the programs made available by Franklin Roosevelt's New Deal. He ar-

bitrarily started handing out jobs made possible under the terms of the New Deal. This got him into
trouble with Washington and even more so with
other Puerto Rican senators, particularly those in the
opposing Conservative Party. Strong-minded, and
sure of himself, Muñoz did not give an inch. He
went on doing his best for the jobless, whatever the
consequences.

When Muñoz softened his stand for independence, it opened the door for an extremely radical
group which made violent demands for independence. At the rallies, riots and violence erupted. In
1936 the new police chief of San Juan was mur-
dered. The assassins were quickly caught and, just
as quickly, executed without benefit of a trial.

In 1937 a parade for independence was scheduled for Ponce. The parade began with complete
police protection. During the progress of the parade,
a single shot came out of the blue. This was followed
by multiple bursts of gunfire that killed twenty people and injured more than one hundred. Soon after
this massacre at Ponce, Muñoz cut himself off from
any connection with the Liberals and formed the
Popular Democratic Party.

Muñoz had clear objectives as he developed his
new party. Members of both the Puerto Rican Senate
and House of Delegates were not answerable to the
average citizen. The candidates literally paid for
their votes with money received from the wealthy
sugar and coffee plantation owners, who lived in
the United States. The legislature needed a complete
overhauling. Another major aim was land reform.
The existing law that decreed no one person could
own more than 500 acres had to be enforced.

Muñoz campaigned throughout the island for
the election of men running for legislative seats on

the Popular Democratic Party ticket. Driving a car between cities, riding horseback into remote inland and mountain villages, he covered most of the 700 voting districts of Puerto Rico. His slogan was "Bread, Land, and Liberty." Wherever he went—in the cities or in rural areas—Muñoz spoke person-to-person in a language his listeners could understand.

Muñoz's most difficult times were spent talking to the jobless in the cities and the peasants on the plantations. These citizens had always accepted two dollars in exchange for their vote. Arguing with the simple declaration that selling his vote had not helped the needy man one bit, Muñoz would tell his listeners that since their vote actually brought them nothing, they should back the Popular Democratic Party. If the party failed to keep its promises, then they could vote them out of office in the next election.

An important event brought Muñoz luck months before the 1940 election. In May, the United States Supreme Court decreed that the 500-acre law was constitutional, and that Puerto Rican officials had the right to enforce it.

When the election was held, the Popular Democratic Party won control of the Puerto Rican legislature, and Muñoz was elected president of the Puerto Rican Senate. He became the most powerful man on the island. To wield his new power and accomplish his objectives successfully depended on the new governor being sent from Washington. Luis Muñoz Marín could only wait and hope.

5
THE
MUÑOZ ERA

Luis Muñoz Marín was deeply concerned when the new governor arrived. He was Rexford G. Tugwell, who had been part of President Franklin Roosevelt's inner circle.

After his appointment and before he officially became governor, Tugwell had visited Puerto Rico. He had traveled the entire island, visiting the coastal areas and the interior. He had seen for himself the deplorable conditions, the need for housing, the low standard of living, the plight of thousands of lower and middle class people without jobs and without sufficient food. They were the same needs that Luis Muñoz Marín was now telling him needed to be taken care of.

The two men, both strong and opinionated, often clashed, yet they maintained an abiding respect for each other. Initially, they agreed that land reform was the most important way to put Puerto Rico on its feet. Then, just as quickly, both came to the conclusion that land reform had to wait. More important at the moment was the need to create jobs for the thousands of unemployed.

Muñoz decided that to create jobs he would first have to build facilities in which people could work producing products that could be sold. So in 1942 Muñoz established the Puerto Rico Development Company, which, he felt certain, had to exist without any interference from the government. The government's only role would be to provide the money. Muñoz appointed Teodoro Moscosco, a brilliant young man from Ponce, as chief operating officer of this new company.

Moscosco created a plan that tied government and industry together in a way that was contrary to how things were done on the mainland. In the United States, the government did not own factories or market products. Moscosco wanted the Puerto Rican government to build and operate factories. The factories, using raw materials available in Puerto Rico—sand, clay, sugarcane—would produce items that could be sold in the United States and elsewhere.

Governor Muñoz approved Moscosco's plan quickly. They named it "Operation Bootstrap." The term implied an effort on the part of the Puerto Ricans to reach down and pull themselves up out of trouble through their own efforts, by using available resources and making the most of them. There were many empty buildings throughout the island. Some were in sugarcane-growing regions, others in coffee- and tobacco-growing areas. The government would prepare the buildings for use. There were no difficulties in finding people to staff the new factories.

☆ **49** ☆

History played a major role in the early successes of Moscosco's Puerto Rico Development Company. When the Japanese bombed Pearl Harbor on December 7, 1941, the Development Company got off on the right foot. With the United States involved in World War II, most U.S. factories were busy making military products. One of the things the United States faced was a liquor shortage. Puerto Rico stepped in to produce rum, the bottles to hold the rum, and the cartons in which the bottled rum could be shipped.

World War II had other effects on the economy of Puerto Rico. Many young Puerto Ricans were drafted into the military, which eased the drastic unemployment problem. Because of Puerto Rico's strategic position at the eastern end of the Caribbean, the United States established military bases on the island. This meant appreciable income from the thousands of men stationed there. Countless jobs were also created for Puerto Ricans to work on the bases.

The plan known as Operation Bootstrap proved to be a profitable one for the duration of the war. Excise taxes alone from the rum shipments brought in over $150 million during the more than five years of the program's duration. However, once the war ended and mainland industries returned to normal, the rum shipments all but ended. Puerto Rico needed more than a quick fix. Its problems were far too deep.

Muñoz explained the problem in simple terms. "Imagine that the population of the whole world . . . should move to the United States. Then the United States would have 650 inhabitants per square mile, the same as Puerto Rico. Imagine that most industrial plants had ceased to operate, that there were no coal mines, no oil wells, no water power. If all this came about, the United States would be in the same position as Puerto Rico was before we decided to do something about it."[1]

That "something" was a new plan to lure American business and manufacturing to the island. Puerto Rico certainly had many features to appeal to American businesspeople. For one thing, there was the importance to business of cheap labor. For another, products made in Puerto Rico could be sold at a reasonable price in the American market. There was also the attraction of Puerto Rico's wonderful year-round climate. An added incentive was the fact that because Puerto Rico was part of the United States, no duty had to be paid on products shipped to the mainland.

The original reaction to this new plan among American business interests was lukewarm; so, in 1947, an incentive too good to pass up was added. Thanks to the passage of a new law, income taxes were exempted for up to ten years on any new factory built on the island. This was a stroke of genius. Within six years, more than 175 new factories were built in Puerto Rico.

That Luis Muñoz Marín had done a magnificent job was finally recognized by the United States Congress. The Senators and Representatives finally decided that Puerto Rico was an asset, not a liability. Therefore, in 1947, Puerto Rico was granted permission to choose its own governor. During an island-wide election in 1948, Luis Muñoz Marín was elected by a wide margin to lead Puerto Rico. No one stood a chance against the wisest, most important man on the island.

Not everyone was happy, however. Although Muñoz had always favored economic independence, those who preferred complete separation from the United States caused violent riots that were quickly suppressed. One bloody outbreak by the pro-independence group resulted in twenty-nine deaths. This took place soon after the election. At about the same time, an assassination attempt by three Puerto Rican men against President Harry Truman was thwarted in Washington.

The years Muñoz had spent in Washington and New York had given him a deep respect for democracy and multiparty politics. He stressed both concepts every time he spoke to Puerto Rican audiences. He encouraged opposition parties to run against his own, and even had a law passed that helped opposition groups get funding from the government for election campaigns.

Moscosco, under the direction of Luis Muñoz Marín, also worked for Puerto Rico's future. In 1949, when the two men became concerned with the poverty and slums that might discourage visiting businessmen, they turned away from building only factories. To give San Juan a new image, the modern and luxurious Caribe Hilton Hotel was built at a cost of $7 million.

Architecturally modern, the multistory hotel gave significance and beauty to the San Juan skyline. It served its original purpose in pleasing American businessmen coming to check on their industrial complexes on the island. It also was the spur which began to attract tourists from the United States, Canada, and Europe. It was the greatest success for Luis Muñoz Marín and the Puerto Rico Development Company.

The following year, after selling off its cement, carton, and glass factories, the Development Company took on a new, more important identity. The

☆ **52** ☆

Puerto Rican legislature made it an arm of the government and renamed it the Puerto Rico Economic Development Administration. Its new function was to bring more and more American investors to the island. Moscosco kept his post as head of the agency, but he was still under the supervision of Luis Muñoz Marín.

With most matters under control, and since he was firmly entrenched as Puerto Rico's elected governor, Muñoz believed it was time to make clear his hopes for Puerto Rico's future status. Formerly an avowed believer in independence for the island, he now explained that he thought it was to the island's benefit to maintain its status as an American dependent. Obviously, the majority of Puerto Ricans agreed with him—Muñoz and his Popular Democratic Party were returned to office three times in succession. As a result of his backing and power, Muñoz was able to resist the protests of the pro-statehood and pro-independence groups.

Most Puerto Ricans were jubilant to see the island's economy improving and prospects for self-government almost at hand. But not the Nationalist Party, led by a revolutionary named Albizu Campos. Campos, scheduled to make a speech at Puerto Rico University, was denied permission by university authorities. In retaliation, the students rioted angrily and went on strike, all to no avail.

Campos and the Nationalist Party soon received another blow at the hands of the United States Congress and President Harry Truman. Pleased with the Muñoz record and trying to strengthen his hand, Congress passed a bill enabling Puerto Rico to hold a Constitutional Convention if voters approved. The Constitution as finally written would, of course, need approval by the American legislators.

☆ **53** ☆

The Nationalist Party protested vehemently, calling the bill a treasonous act aimed at killing independence for Puerto Rico. The group that favored making Puerto Rico a state of the United States also protested, but on a less vocal scale.

On October 28, 1950, members of the Nationalist group raided Puerto Rico's Rio Piedras prison, killing two guards and helping one hundred prisoners to escape. Two days later, four of Campos's followers stormed Governor Muñoz's mansion in San Juan. The four were intercepted by police and all four rebels and one policeman were killed in the gun battle. Later that same day, another contingent of Nationalists invaded and occupied the police compound at Jayuya. During the next two days, police had to fight Nationalists in four other Puerto Rican towns, including Ponce.

Governor Muñoz called out the National Guard and declared that all of Puerto Rico was under martial law. The National Guard had little trouble in defeating the revolutionaries, although one National Guardsman was killed and seven were wounded. The cost to the Nationalists was eighteen dead and eleven wounded. The overall casualty list for the three-day October uprising was twenty-nine dead, and fifty-one injured.

The Nationalists had suffered a bitter defeat but were not wiped out. On November 1, 1950, two Nationalists made their way to Washington. Their aim was the assassination of President Harry Truman. The terrorists were no more successful than their compatriots had been during the October uprising in San Juan. One of the two Nationalists was killed; the other, Oscar Collazo, was wounded. Collazo was later tried in Washington and sentenced to death.

The morning after the aborted assassination attempt, all Nationalist Party leaders, including Campos, were rounded up by San Juan police. Tried in court and found guilty, Campos was sentenced to serve seventy-nine years in jail. (He served less than three years, for on September 30, 1953, feeling compassion for Campos's age and ill health, Governor Muñoz granted him a pardon.)

June 4, 1951, was a red-letter day for Muñoz and Puerto Rico. The year before, President Truman signed the bill granting Puerto Rico the right to write its own constitution; it was now time for the islanders to vote. Muñoz backers walked away with 81 percent of the vote and plans were formulated for a constitutional convention.

The islanders voted for members of the convention who would write the constitution. Of the ninety-two delegates elected, seventy were from Muñoz's Popular Democratic Party. Statehood proponents numbered only fifteen, and seven delegates favored independence.

It took from September 17, 1951, until February 6, 1952, to develop the Puerto Rican Constitution. The document, which was similar to the United States Constitution, would keep Puerto Rico a Commonwealth of the United States.

President Truman reviewed the document and sent it to Congress for analysis. It was found that Muñoz and the constitutional convention had gone a bit too far. In the Puerto Rican Bill of Rights, for example, it would grant Puerto Ricans protections not available under the United States Constitution. Congress made a few revisions and sent it back for island approval. When this was accomplished, Puerto Rico was at last ready to govern itself as a Commonwealth of the United States of America.

☆ 55 ☆

On the morning of July 25, 1952, the melodious chime of church bells began a day-long celebration for Puerto Rico's new status as a Commonwealth of the United States. Governor Luis Muñoz Marín raised the Puerto Rican flag and proclaimed a new way of life for the islanders. Celebrities, officials from the mainland and Puerto Rico, reporters, and visitors joined in morning and afternoon ceremonies of speeches and congratulations. The night echoed with music, songs, and dancing from San Juan to Ponce.

With the fall of 1952 only months away, Muñoz busied himself with day-to-day responsibilities as well as preparations for the important November election. Though his election as the first governor of the Commonwealth seemed certain, he believed there was no sense in taking chances. Besides, keeping the Popular Democratic Party in control of both houses of the legislature was as important as his own re-election.

Whenever the opportunity presented itself, Muñoz traveled to some different place on the island, being particularly careful to impress the peasants with the importance of the election. All in all, it proved to be a difficult campaign. The two opposing parties, one pressuring for statehood and the other violently clamoring for independence, pressured Muñoz through all three months.

When the votes were counted in November, Luis Muñoz Marín was elected the first governor of the Commonwealth of Puerto Rico by 65 percent of the electorate. When the votes for legislative seats were counted, Muñoz had all but a stranglehold on the four years ahead. His Popular Democratic Party swamped the others. It won twenty-three out of thirty-two seats in the Senate and forty-seven out of sixty-four in the House. The independence group won only five seats in the Senate and ten in the House. The statehood coalition didn't do as well, winning just four seats in the Senate and seven in the House of Representatives.

The next three elections were no different. Each time, Muñoz and the legislature returned to office with the same proportion of votes for the Popular Democratic Party. Muñoz did all the thinking, sending bills to the legislature and receiving almost automatic approval. Even the minority parties gave him no trouble. More often than not, they voted as Muñoz wanted the vote to go.

The one thing Muñoz could not control, however, was the violence that marked the independence group's actions during his entire time in office. In March 1954, four members of the Nationalist Party stormed the House of Representatives in Washington. Without warning, they fired random shots at the Congressmen in session. Five Congressmen were injured. Following an investigation, seventeen Nationalists were put on trial, and eventually fourteen were convicted of conspiracy.

When Alaska was admitted as the forty-ninth state in 1958, the Puerto Ricans favoring statehood stepped up their campaign. Knowing that the American government would be turned off by any violence, they began peaceful demonstrations to achieve their goal. They picked up even more steam the following year when Hawaii became America's fiftieth state.

The never-ending, three-sided debate—over statehood, independence, and maintaining the status quo as a commonwealth—desperately needed some resolution. Muñoz turned to Washington, and Congress helped by setting up a United States and

Puerto Rico Commission to resolve the matter. In 1966 the commission decided that only an island-wide vote by the people could provide an answer.

The Puerto Rico legislature ordered a vote in 1967 to determine the will of the majority. Whatever the result, it would have no real bearing since the United States Congress had to approve whatever plan the Puerto Rican people came up with. Was it to be independence? Was it to become the fifty-first state? Or should Puerto Rico remain as it was, a Commonwealth answerable to the United States?

Even though Commonwealth status won by a substantial majority, the election decided nothing. Most of those in favor of independence failed to vote, but independence leaders claimed they had actually won since the nonvoters plus those who did vote for independence would have brought about a total greater than the commonwealth vote.

Pleased with the results of the vote, Muñoz Marín was disturbed by the constant bickering over independence, statehood, and Commonwealth status. There were far more important issues relating to Puerto Rico's future, he believed—the issues of poverty, jobs, the education of the children, and the building of adequate schools, for example. But the question of the status of the island continued to dominate the interests of Puerto Ricans, wealthy and poor alike.

The seeming indifference of the American Congress regarding the status issue was also puzzling. It had created the Commonwealth, but never indicated whether it was merely a temporary condition. Some definite decision by Congress, one way or another, would have brought some stability to the continuing three-way fight.

The answer could lie in the fact that Americans

did not understand the Puerto Ricans. American politicians and ordinary tourists had come to the island many times, but most, if not all, had not looked beyond the surface. Few were aware of the Puerto Ricans' abiding love for their Spanish heritage and culture, a cherished commodity they did not want to lose. Muñoz thought he had made that abundantly clear when he ordered that Spanish would be the official language of the Commonwealth.

There was considerable debate over which language—English or Spanish—should be taught in Puerto Rican public schools and what the significance of each should be. The answer was perhaps best expressed by Ismael Rodriguez Bou, an influential educational leader. He defined the contrary judgments of the statehood and independence proponents, relative to the language choice, in somewhat simple terms:

> Those in favor of English as the language of instruction were identified as American assimilationists, and those in favor of Spanish as separationists. To this day the teaching of English has never been able to free itself from a certain political involvement.[2]

The United States kept Puerto Rico guessing in many other ways during the process of Americanization. Washington had made it clear from the first days of occupation that unless Puerto Ricans were "Americanized," they would not be eligible to enjoy the same benefits as residents in the fifty states. But exactly what was meant by Americanization was never made clear.

Governor Luis Muñoz Marín firmly believed that teaching English to Puerto Rican students was beneficial to their future. However, he did not believe that Spanish should be ignored. It was vital that the Spanish heritage and culture be maintained. It seemed strange, though, that in more than twenty years no American government official had voiced any precise thinking on the subject.

In the late 1930s, President Franklin Delano Roosevelt had expressed some concern. In a letter to Jose Gallardo, the man he had appointed as Puerto Rico's Commissioner of Education, Roosevelt wrote in part, "I desire at this time to make clear the attitude of my administration on the extremely important matter of teaching English in Puerto Rico." In ending his letter, the president wrote: "Moreover, it is only through familiarity with our language that the Puerto Ricans will be able to take full advantage of the economic opportunities which became available to them when they were made American citizens."[3]

While American government officials continued to stress the importance of using English textbooks as a means of Americanizing Puerto Ricans, prominent educators looked beyond the surface at the underlying issues. Dr. Algernon Coleman, Professor of French at the University of Chicago, visited Puerto Rico in 1939 and analyzed the situation for himself. He was so disturbed by what he found that he sent a letter to Secretary of the Interior Harold Ickes. He wrote, in part:

There has been much talk of an educational program whereby the children of the island ought to be made really bilingual. Such a purpose seems wholly unreal to one who is so little expert in these matters. We know, for example, what has been the outcome of the

☆ **60** ☆

long time effort of the British to accomplish this in India. Spanish will continue to be the mother tongue of all Puerto Ricans. . . . Few of our theorists on the subject seem to realize the small numbers of opportunities that most Puerto Ricans have for speaking English in any continuous fashion as a genuine vehicle of intercourse with others.

It seems to me that too little attention has been given to formulating and applying useful criteria for choosing textbooks in most Puerto Rico schools. . . .[4]

Dr. Coleman's judgment was backed up by a report issued by the Institute of Field Studies at Columbia University's Teachers College. After a lengthy visit to Puerto Rico to consider the matter, a report was issued which observed, "Puerto Rican children spend much time reading about little boys and girls in the United States riding tricycles, playing in boats, and having luxurious doll houses in spacious playrooms. At the only time during which thousands of the children will have an opportunity to learn how to live better lives in Puerto Rico, they are spending long hours of each school year reading about haystacks, steam shovels, skating on ice and sliding down hills in snow. . . ."[5]

Such opinions by credible educational experts matched the expressed feelings of Governor Muñoz. It remained his belief that Puerto Ricans should keep their Spanish culture and heritage alive. He did, however, permit the teaching of English in private schools, most of which were taught by American Catholic nuns. Spanish continued as the official language in elementary and secondary public schools.

There were factors other than language which

contributed to the Americanization of Puerto Rico. There were the seventeen military training bases occupied by both Americans and Puerto Ricans. Military discipline and training helped influence Americanization. The Puerto Ricans in training at these bases could not help but absorb American ways and values.

There was also another plus, one that worked both ways. Not only did Americanization bring the glories and opportunities of the United States to Puerto Rico, it also increased and made solid Puerto Rico's pride in itself and its people. Throughout his many years as governor, Muñoz Marín had backed all efforts of the people of Puerto Rico to participate in and improve their talents in cultural and athletic endeavors. Music and the performing arts were encouraged in high schools. Athletic fields for all ages were created and maintained.

With facilities available, young Puerto Ricans took advantage of opportunities. Many who were born on the island made great names for themselves on the mainland and brought their fame back to their homeland. There was the great Broadway actor, Jose Ferrer, also noted for his work in motion pictures and television. Also known for her achievement in films and television is the actress Rita Moreno.

Bringing Puerto Rico international acclaim in the area of classical music was the Classic Musical Festival. Still held annually, it was organized in 1957 by Pablo Casals, perhaps the most accomplished cellist in musical history. Casals was also the conductor and director of the Puerto Rico Symphony Orchestra. Among many others, the name of Jose Feliciano, a blind singer with an extraordinary voice, is very familiar to American music lovers.

Sports also played a major role in acquainting the world with Puerto Rican abilities. With the support of American-educated Governor Muñoz, Puerto Rico became an island of sports fanatics. Names familiar to most Americans and sports enthusiasts throughout the world became recognized as outstanding performers in almost every sports activity known.

In boxing, Sixto Escobar won the world bantamweight championship twice. Carlos Ortiz became junior welterweight champion in 1959. In golf, Chi Chi Rodriguez was one of the top performers on American courses. On the tennis courts, Charles Pasarell was top-ranked among all American amateurs in 1968.

Even before its status as a Commonwealth of the United States, Puerto Rico had entered international competitions. While not always winning, its athletes showed themselves as performers with a future. Puerto Rico entered such spectaculars as an independent country, not as a colony or possession of the United States. In the decade of the 1930s, the island took part in the Central American and the Caribbean games. One decade later, Puerto Rico took part in the International Olympics.

In 1966 the little island showed itself as a force to be reckoned with in international games. Backed enthusiastically by Muñoz, no longer governor but a member of the Puerto Rico Senate, Puerto Rico took an $8 million chance in hosting the Central American and Caribbean games. It was a courageous step for the financially strapped country. Dubbed Puerto Rico's greatest spectacle, it not only was a success financially but also brought increased recognition of future growth.

Puerto Rico did not win anything, but the world

☆ **63** ☆

looked upon its performance as a moral victory. It had placed second to Mexico, a nation with eighteen times more people from which to draw its athletes. During the games, a Puerto Rican swimmer, Ann Lallande, established a record for the games by winning ten gold and two bronze medals.

It is in baseball, however, that Puerto Rican pride shines brightest. Luis Muñoz Marín's own Americanization in Washington and New York had made him aware of the potential opportunities for young Puerto Rican males in professional baseball. As a result, almost from the very beginning of his tenure as governor, Muñoz had approved the development of baseball diamonds throughout the island. The next step was the organization of leagues in which boys of all ages could take part.

Six professional baseball teams on the island have produced many players who have thrilled spectators at minor and major league stadiums in the United States and Canada. First to make it to the major leagues from Puerto Rico was Hiram Bithorn, who succeeded with the Chicago Cubs of the National League in 1946. Others who followed to teams in both major leagues included Felix Millan, Ruben Gomez, and Jose Pagan. The most spectacular of Puerto Rican baseball stars, and ones with names familiar to all baseball fans, were Roberto Clemente and Orlando Cepeda.

Undeniably, Luis Muñoz Marín had shown America and the world that Puerto Rico was a viable nation. In recognition of his accomplishments, the United States awarded him the Presidential Medal of Freedom in 1963. Then, with the 1964 election just months away, Muñoz made a bold decision. Telling his Popular Democratic leaders that Puerto Ricans

For four centuries, Spain looked upon Puerto Rico
as one of its more important colonial territories.
In 1898, a Cuban revolt brought on the Spanish-
American War. This photo shows the bombard-
ment of San Juan, Puerto Rico.

Juan Ponce de Leon, the Spanish explorer
who established the first settlement on the
Puerto Rico mainland

A strange and cruel mixture of religious
zeal and greed characterized Spanish
treatment of the peoples of the Caribbean
islands. Spaniards considered the natives
subhuman, fit only for manual labor.

Ramon Betances preached revolution,
independence from Spain, and an end
to Spanish oppression.

Hope welled in the hearts of many Puerto Ricans as the United States took possession of the island after the United States' victory in the Spanish-American War.

Luis Muñoz Rivera, poet, scholar, astute politician, and leader of the island's Autonomist Party

Startling contrasts in school and housing conditions:

Typical rural school lunchroom in the early 1900s.
It was built with private funds at a cost of $74.00.

The lunchroom of one of the modern San Juan schools, built during Franklin D. Roosevelt's New Deal. The Puerto Rico Reconstruction Administration was set up then to construct new buildings, modernize old ones, clear blighted areas, and build new factories.

Eleanor Roosevelt visiting a Puerto Rican
resident. Note the poor housing conditions.

Youngsters playing baseball in front
of a new housing settlement in 1938

A typical farmer, shown bringing home sugarcane cuttings to feed his cows. This is the "common" man for whom Roosevelt's program had been organized.

These farmers have been taught the art of
diversification of crops.

It's wash day for these Jibaros—hill people of Puerto Rico—and the women do their laundry as the children swim in the river. These are the people Luis Muñoz Marín hoped to lift from poverty by breaking down vote buying in the island.

Luis Muñoz Marín (left), senate president of Puerto Rico, confers with Rexford G. Tugwell, President Roosevelt's envoy to Puerto Rico, who became governor of the island in 1941. Marín succeeded him in 1948 as the first elected governor of the island.

In November 1950, Puerto Rican Nationalists, calling for complete independence from the United States, moved in to take over a mountain town. They also made an abortive attempt to assassinate President Harry Truman in Washington. After this incident, San Juan police rounded up all Nationalist Party leaders. Here National Guardsmen move in to take control of the town of Jayuya.

On July 25, 1952, Puerto Rico celebrated
its new status as a commonwealth of the
United States. Troops and guests take part
in ceremonies at El Morro Fortress.

One of the many baseball teams organized during the early years of Luis Muñoz Marín's governorship. Puerto Rican pride shines brightest when it extols the talents of the many great baseball heroes from the island.

Thousands of advocates of independence
for Puerto Rico march through San Juan's
tourist district in 1973, protesting the presence
of United States mayors gathered for a
conference. The protesters also demanded
the release of "political prisoners" from
mainland federal jails and political separation
of the island from the United States.

Facing page: Politics in Puerto Rico is a passion:
Not merely a civic duty, it's more like war or religion.
(Top) Governor Hernandez Colón campaigns for
reelection in September 1976. (Bottom) Colón's
opponent, San Juan mayor Carlos Romero Barcelo
of the pro-statehood New Progressive Party,
defeated Colón and became governor in 1977.

Thousands of pro-independence demonstrators
march in front of Puerto Rico's capitol in
San Juan during the 1989 U.S. congressional
hearings on the island's status.

should begin to realize they could not continue to depend on one man, he announced that he would not seek a fifth term as governor. Instead, he would run for his old seat in the island Senate.

Believing that Puerto Rico was not yet ready for statehood, and fearing another uprising by the Independent Nationalists, Muñoz insisted on selecting his own successor. He chose another member of the Popular Democratic Party, the island Secretary of State, Roberto Sanchez Viella. Viella was elected governor and Muñoz returned to the Senate.

6
THE
YEARS
AFTER MUÑOZ

On January 3, 1965, Luis Muñoz Marín gave up the governorship of his beloved Puerto Rico. It was a sad day for the countless Puerto Ricans who had elected him four times. Muñoz had been held in very high regard not only by his people but also by the president and Congress of the United States.

Muñoz had accomplished much in bringing some sense of stability to the island Commonwealth. Though many problems remained, he was leaving the island in far better shape than when he originally took over. Perhaps his greatest accomplishment was Operation Bootstrap, which had helped raise the per capita income of the island from a meager $250 to $1,500 annually.

It was deep concern for Puerto Rico's future that brought about Muñoz's decision not to seek another term as governor. Nearing seventy years of age, he realized he had just a few years left. While he held

☆ **66** ☆

power, no other man within the Popular Democratic Party had emerged as a viable individual to carry on. Roberto Sanchez Viella, as secretary of state, seemed the best possible choice, which was why Muñoz campaigned so hard for Viella's election.

Muñoz realized that Viella was still a question mark, so he decided to accept the leadership of the Puerto Rican Senate rather than go into total retirement. Muñoz was also determined to give Viella every possible chance to govern without interference from him. Muñoz kept a low profile during the first two years of Viella's term. He attended few meetings, spending most of his time either at his home outside San Juan or in Washington at Puerto Rico Commission meetings.

During those first two years, 1965 and 1966, Governor Sanchez Viella held quite firmly to the principles of the Popular Democratic Party as set down by Luis Muñoz Marín. More factories were built under the Operation Bootstrap umbrella. As a result, the number of people working was at least the same as the number unemployed. And the per capita income began edging toward $2,000 per year. By the end of 1966, Roberto Sanchez Viella was riding high, a worthy successor to the great Luis Muñoz Marín.

The Sanchez aura faded though, early the following year. This was not due to his work as governor, but rather to problems in his personal life. Early in 1967, it became evident that Sanchez Viella was not only ignoring his duties as governor but also neglecting his wife and famly. The reason was one of his staff aides, Jeanette Ramos, the daughter of Ernesto Ramos Antonini, Puerto Rico's most prominent black political personality, who had served as speaker of the House of Representatives until he died in 1963.

☆ **67** ☆

To make matters even worse for himself, Viella was never accompanied by his wife in public, but rather by the glamorous and politically ambitious Jeanette Ramos. This angered the Puerto Ricans, most of whom were straightlaced Roman Catholics. The public reaction made no difference to Viella.

But the mounting criticism did finally begin to affect Sanchez Viella's conscience. To justify himself, he began bad-mouthing the platform of the Popular Democratic Party. During interviews with newspaper, radio, and television reporters, he also made pointed remarks designed to blame Muñoz Marín for his problems. Many of his statements, made no doubt to evoke some sympathy, mentioned his intention to resign. Also, his remarks often insinuated that the Commonwealth status was perhaps not best for Puerto Rico, and that independence might well be better for the island's future.

The thinly veiled inferences about possible independence brought about a horrendous spring and summer. It gave the violent faction of those favoring independence all they needed to initiate months of terror during 1967. Independence fanatics began an almost endless series of bombings aimed at anything American. Banks, factories, stores, supermarkets, and gas stations were all targets. Fortunately, there were few casualties, but millions of dollars' worth of damage was done. The only safe installations were American military bases protected by American soldiers.

Puerto Ricans were further upset with their governor for doing little or nothing to stop the countless explosions which rocked the small island. Governor Sanchez Viella, they believed, was far too busy arranging his personal affairs. On September 28, 1967, Viella divorced his wife of some thirty years.

On September 30, he married Jeanette Ramos and took her on a honeymoon to Washington.

Selecting Washington for his wedding trip proved to be a serious mistake for Viella. When he attended a meeting of the Puerto Rico Presidential Commission, of which he was a member, he found himself berated by other commissioners on a number of points. He was questioned about his failure to control the independence group. The other commissioners also demanded proof of the many derogatory statements Viella had made against Luis Muñoz Marín.

Governor Sanchez Viella could give no answer to questions about the bombing of American facilities on the island. As for his comments about Muñoz, he first denied making any such accusations. Then, shown reprints of statements he had made, he merely offered an apology. He left Washington and returned to Puerto Rico.

Back on the island and embittered by his treatment by the Presidential Commission, Sanchez Viella considered his options. Prodded by his new wife, who loved the glory of being First Lady, he decided not to resign. Nor would he be only a one-term governor. He was firmly determined to run for re-election in 1968.

To prepare himself for the campaign, as well as to rebuild ruined political fences, he was determined to appeal to the people. Though he never relished public speaking appearances, he made plans to travel throughout the island. The great concern was whether Puerto Ricans would come to hear him after all the unpleasant publicity.

Puerto Ricans did flock to hear Sanchez Viella's speeches whenever they were scheduled in their communities. Most, however, did not come to hear what he had to say; they came to stare at glamorous

☆ **69** ☆

Jeanette Ramos Sanchez, always meticulously and fashionably dressed and beaming smiles at the audience. Those who came to listen and judge went away confused, unable to understand where Sanchez Viella stood on any issue. They also could not figure out whether he favored Commonwealth status as the Popular Democratic Party did or if he was in favor of statehood or independence.

Long before the governor made his speechmaking tour, Luis Muñoz Marín had returned to his Senate seat on a full-time basis. He was very worried over the possible collapse of the Popular Democratic Party at the hands of Sanchez Viella. The former governor came back determined to be a thorn in Viella's side—and he was exactly that.

In early January of 1968, before the governor could give his annual State of the Commonwealth message to the Puerto Rican Congress, Muñoz made his own State of the Commonwealth report. Four days later, Sanchez Viella gave his speech to the combined House and Senate. In it he charged Muñoz with trying to upset and capture the powers of the governor.

The result was to be an all-out fight between the sitting governor of Puerto Rico and his predecessor. Viella wasted no time. On March 28, 1968, he announced that he would definitely be a candidate for re-election as governor. Muñoz then released a statement declaring that it was "impossible for me to give my support again to Roberto Sanchez Viella."[1]

It was expected that without the support of his own party that Sanchez Viella would gracefully bow out and not seek another term, but he did not do this. Instead, he fought back, showing himself to be a far different man than the shy, retiring, party loyalist whom Muñoz Marín had nurtured and had made secretary of state. This new Sanchez Viella was perhaps best described by the *New York Times* on March 28, 1968.

The article reported that Viella was one who had "shed the image of the taciturn, darkly brooding man with heavy hornrimmed glasses in favor of a new image of congeniality and even flamboyance."[2] Sanchez Viella was now a battler determined to defeat his former mentor and retain the governorship of Puerto Rico.

At the Popular Democratic Party's 1968 nominating convention held July 21, Sanchez Viella began his quest for a second term as governor by continuing the tirade against Luis Muñoz Marín that he had made in a television address the night before. He then had his name placed in nomination. But two other members of the Popular Democratic Party also entered names of nominees.

Sanchez Viella had done so badly in trying to impress the party delegates that it took only one ballot to defeat him. He received a meager 102 votes. Negron Lopez got 1,126 and Polanco Abreu, 475. Lopez was declared the Popular Democratic Party candidate for governor.

Sanchez Viella stubbornly refused to give up. Two weeks after the convention, a pro-statehood organization known as the People's Party asked him to take control and become their nominee for governor. He accepted. This opened the door to a wild three-way battle for the governorship of Puerto Rico.

Luis Ferré, a wealthy industrialist from Ponce, decided to take advantage of the rift in the Popular Democratic Party. Head of an organization called the Statehood Party, he realized that he would need to change his outward insistence that Puerto Rico should become America's fifty-first state. A vote taken the year before had shown an overwhelming desire by Puerto Ricans to remain a Commonwealth of the United States. In addition, Sanchez Viella had joined the statehood forces. Ferré accordingly removed any obstacles to his chances by changing the name of his political group from the Statehood Party to the People's Progressive Party and then to the New Progressive Party. He entered the race for governor, campaigning on a pledge to improve government services.

The campaign was the most bitter of the six elections since Puerto Rico was granted the right to govern itself. Ferré attacked both other candidates. They, in turn, berated Ferré and each other. The fourth, and most powerful, voice in the hotly contested campaign was that of Luis Muñoz Marín.

Unfortunately for the Popular Democratic Party, Muñoz spent far more time and effort in defeating Viella as a traitor to the principles of the Popular Democrats than in promoting Negron, his own party candidate. The result was the first defeat for the Popular Democrats. Luis Ferré was elected governor by some 25,000 votes. Roberto Sanchez Viella ran a distant third.

Once the election was finalized, Luis Muñoz Marín left Puerto Rico for Spain, where he was to live out his life and write his memoirs. He left behind a Puerto Rico shaped by his own brilliant mind, one that would retain its Spanish heritage and yet be a Commonwealth of the United States.

Luis Ferré served only one term as governor of Puerto Rico. His New Progressive Party did take control of the House of Representatives, but the Popular Democrats retained supremacy in the Senate, so he had little chance of putting any possible reforms into practice. His position was further weakened because almost immediately after taking office, he returned to his position that statehood was Puerto Rico's only real future.

This quick turnaround in his position infuriated the groups fighting for independence, many of whom had voted for him. Ferré's four years in office were marked by months of riots by pro-independence partisans. From San Juan to Ponce and from Caparra to Mayaguez, explosions shattered the peace of Puerto Rico. American installations throughout the island were the targets of inflamed passions.

When Luis Muñoz Marín left for Spain, he left the future of the Popular Democratic Party in the hands of his trusted friend, Rafael Hernández Colón. Colón did as Muñoz had hoped. He reorganized the Popular Democratic Party and restored its once invulnerable position. It was Hernández Colón who succeeded Luis Ferré as governor in January 1973.

Hernández Colón's first years as governor proved troublesome through no fault of his own. The worldwide recession of the early 1970s wrecked the slowly improving Puerto Rican economy. Businesses were forced to close their doors. Thousands of Puerto Ricans lost their jobs. Many people who had emigrated to the mainland became unemployed and returned to the island, thus increasing the unemployment problem.

The greatly expanded population meant thousands more mouths which could not be fed. With hunger facing so many, and honest money hard to come by, a wave of crime swept through Puerto Rico. Governor Hernández Colón did the best he could to stem the rising tide of robberies. He tried to get enough government money to pay for the most essential public services, but his hands were tied. The New Progressive Party had lost the governorship, but had taken control of both the Senate and House of Representatives. Forced into a corner, Hernández Colón was never able to install the reforms he hoped would improve the economy and living conditions in Puerto Rico.

In 1976, the New Progressive Party nominated Carlos Romero Barcelo to oppose Hernández Colón. Barcelo, who had been mayor of San Juan for eight years, wisely ignored the New Progressive Party's dedication to statehood and aimed his campaign oratory at the serious plight of the Puerto Rican economy and widespread crime on the island. Barcelo easily defeated Colón and took over the governor's office in January 1977 under ideal circumstances—both the Senate and House of Representatives were controlled by Barcelo's New Progressive Party.

Though everything was in his favor, Barcelo made a serious blunder. Ignoring the fact that the combined votes for the Independence and Commonwealth candidates totaled more than 50,000 above his winning vote, Barcelo resumed his fight for statehood.

Pro-independence hard-liners, many of whom had voted for Barcelo, were furious. American businesses, offices, and installations were attacked again in another rash of bombings. Throughout the island, the cry was heard that Puerto Rico existed only as a colony of the United States and should be given the right to govern itself, as Cuba did. Cuba then added fuel to the fire with a demand that the United Nations investigate America's role in Puerto Rico and that the island be granted independence. The proposal was not successful, but it did make the American public more aware that Puerto Rico was part of the United States.

As a result of the Cuban proposal in the United Nations, and reports of the increased bombing activity on the island, the news media opened American eyes to Puerto Rican problems. Newspapers and radio and television began carrying stories. Magazines featured articles about the island's difficulties. Perhaps most enlightening was a broadcast on August 28, 1977, by the CBS program "60 Minutes," within a week of one of the most destructive bombings by independence fanatics.

The Puerto Rico reported on in the program in late August 1977 was a far cry from the proud Commonwealth fashioned by Luis Muñoz Marín. While the per capita income had continued to rise slowly throughout the decade, Puerto Rico sank more and more to the status of a welfare state increasingly dependent on the United States treasury. In the nearly eighty years since the United States came to Puerto Rico, it has spent more than $600 billion to shore up the island economy. Year after year, food stamp lines have lengthened, so that by mid-1977 the food stamp cost for Puerto Rico reached an outlay of $600 million.

Unfortunately, while the United States has helped Puerto Rico tremendously, it has done little to help the island stand by itself. The fertile land should be able to grow most of its own food products, yet almost everything is imported from the United States. This enriches American businesses but destroys Puerto Rico's ability to provide for itself.

Puerto Rico's economy remained stagnant despite Governor Barcelo's attempts to improve it. Further marring his first term in office was a scandal in which two young pro-independence radicals were killed by the police, a tragic incident that Barcelo was accused of covering up. Nonetheless, Barcelo

☆ 75 ☆

was elected for a second term in November 1980, narrowly defeating Hernández Colón's bid to resume the governorship.

Though he was unable to improve the Puerto Rican economy or control the violence of the pro-Independence radicals, Carlos Romero Barcelo tried for a third term as governor. In the election held November 6, 1984, he was defeated by Rafael Hernández Colón. Colón not only took back the governor's chair, but he came back into office with his Popular Democratic Party controlling two-thirds of the seats in both houses of the island legislature.

A turnaround in the Puerto Rican economy, slow as it was, began within months after Hernández and the Popular Democratic Party resumed control. Once the party that favored no immediate change in Puerto Rico's status took over the reins of government, the pro-statehood clamor and violence subsided considerably. Rafael Hernández Colón and the two houses of the legislature were able to initiate reforms to ease the food stamp lines.

A more peaceful Puerto Rico then brought about a rise in tourism, which brought millions of dollars to the struggling Puerto Rican treasury. This renewed hope for Puerto Rico's future helped Hernández Colón and his Popular Democrats win re-election in November 1988. Six months after Hernández Colón was elected, the growth rate of the economy was a surprising 14.8 percent. Within ten months, however, nature temporarily stemmed the euphoria. Hurricane Hugo, which had hit other areas of the Caribbean the day before, lashed the San Juan vicinity on September 18, 1989. Six people were killed and 57,000 homes were destroyed. Vicious winds of 140 mph caused $6 billion in damage.

An unrelated tragedy in the wake of Hurricane

Hugo saddened Puerto Ricans far more than the billions of dollars in damage done by the storm. It was the loss of a respected and revered favorite son. Roberto Clemente, the great outfielder of the Pittsburgh Pirates baseball team, a man who loved his native Puerto Rico, died in a plane crash.

Puerto Rico recovered from the destruction of Hurricane Hugo. Its golden beaches were once again crowded, its hotels filled. In the year following Hugo, it is estimated that more than 2 million tourists visited the island, stimulating its still sluggish economy.

With the last decade of the twentieth century well under way, Puerto Rican pride runs high. Americanized or not, its Spanish culture is still strong. During his two terms beginning in 1985, Rafael Hernández Colón and his Popular Democratic Party had restored a sense of stability to Puerto Rico just as his mentor, Luis Muñoz Marín, had done during his four terms. The problem of poverty still existed and food stamp lines were still too long, but the economy did move ahead slowly. As Hernández Colón began his second term in 1989, Puerto Rico's per capita income was over $5,000. While it was still less than the lowest of all fifty American states, Mississippi, it was the highest of any Latin American country.

Meanwhile, the government in Washington was finally giving serious consideration to Puerto Rico as a probable fifty-first state. After his election, President George Bush openly advocated statehood for Puerto Rico. Statehood, however, could come only if a majority of Puerto Ricans wanted it. The results of two previous plebiscites, votes taken in 1952 and 1967, had been to remain a Commonwealth, exempt from federal income taxes. Whatever the majority decided in another vote would determine Puerto Rico's future.

The Energy and Resources Committee of the United States Senate began hearings on Puerto Rico in 1989. This committee, which has jurisdiction over all American territories other than the fifty states, was chaired by Senator Bennett Johnson, Democrat from Louisiana. He and Senator James McClure of Idaho, the ranking Republican member, continued the hearings in San Juan.

Only the statehood proponents warmly welcomed the two senators as they began their hearings in the luxurious Government Reception Building in September 1989. Despite a drenching rainstorm, more than 70,000 backers of independence jeered and shouted obscenities outside the building. Governor Hernández Colón and his Popular Democratic Party quietly resented what they believed to be interference on the part of George Bush and his administration.

The hearings were long, tedious, and frustrating. In the end, only one meaningful decision was made. The senators declared a vote would be taken in 1991. The purpose of that vote would be different from those taken in 1952 and 1967, both of which only determined Puerto Rican reaction to continuing as a Commonwealth and did not offer any alternative. The 1991 vote would specifically offer the choices of independence, statehood, and Commonwealth status as it existed.

The senators returned to Washington to plan for the expected vote. Before the Energy and Resources Committee could get very far with its deliberations, the future of Puerto Rico was forced to take a back seat to exploding world events—the Persian Gulf War, the fight for peace in the Middle East, and the collapse of communism.

☆ **78** ☆

7
WHICH
WILL IT BE?

Nineteen ninety-two has all but passed into history, and Puerto Rico's future remains in limbo. With 1992 an election year in the United States, there is little likelihood of a plebiscite. It will, however, come about sometime and, very likely, before the beginning of the twenty-first century. When the time does come, which of the three roads will Puerto Rico travel?

☆ THE CASE FOR INDEPENDENCE ☆

During the meetings held on the island in 1989, the Energy and Resources Committee of the United States Senate assured Puerto Ricans that if they voted for independence, it would definitely be granted. Puerto Ricans were also told that if independence did come about, all who wished to retain their American citizenship could do so.

The chances for an independent republic of Puerto Rico actually range from slim to none. The decades-long violence and extensive damage done by the more fanatical groups have alienated not only Americans on the mainland but also the average Puerto Rican.

It has been estimated that less than one tenth of the Puerto Rican population favor independence. Perhaps one-third of these *independencitas*, as they are called on the island, make up the more rabid and destructive element. In 1986, it was revealed that a security unit of the Puerto Rican police had compiled a list of 130,000 names of individuals they called "subversives." The list included names of athletes, actors, and active politicians.

Even the moderate pro-statehood and pro-Commonwealth adherents were repelled by what they considered repressive measures that Americans in the states would not have tolerated. The Puerto Rico Civil Rights Commission did begin a series of lengthy hearings. Then David Noriega, a member of the House of Representatives who also belonged to the Independence Party, brought a lawsuit against the Puerto Rico police. In the end, the tactics used to repress Independence Party rights were declared illegal.

So, too, were the actions of the American FBI as they investigated the robbery of the Wells Fargo Bank in Puerto Rico. The FBI agents had tapped the telephones of *independencitas* and recorded hundreds of hours of their conversations. Most tapped phones were those of members of a radical group called *Los Macheteros*, an element considered to be the most dangerous of the *independencitas*.

The virulent and costly destruction brought

about by the more militant *independencitas* seriously damaged the independence movement. It has cost the moderate and law-abiding people who feel strongly about being a free nation a great deal. Far too many of them have been continually harassed as they go about their daily lives. In many instances, they have been denied employment. Since the violent, uncontrollable *independencitas* were only a small minority of those who favored independence, many Puerto Ricans suffered unfairly.

Nonetheless, repression has not slowed the independence movement, which continued to strengthen and grow after the Senate committee assured its proponents they would have an equal say when the three-way vote is taken. But many questions remain on the issue of whether an independent Puerto Rico can exist.

☆ THE CASE FOR CONTINUING ☆ COMMONWEALTH STATUS

Most political experts in Puerto Rico agree that the only viable choices for the island are statehood or remaining as is, that is, a Commonwealth of the United States. Many will tell you that if the vote were taken in either 1993 or 1994, the result would be a decision to remain a Commonwealth.

Continued Commonwealth status for another five, perhaps ten, years is all but certain if the Popular Democratic Party is returned to power for another four-year term. The two previous plebiscites, held fifteen years apart, revealed general satisfaction with the Commonwealth status. And the general elections, held every four years, resulted mainly in victories for the Popular Democrats. Even when the

New Progressive Party won the governorship, the election results were extremely close.

More than forty years have passed since Puerto Rico was granted the right to govern itself. In all that time, beginning with Governor Luis Muñoz Marín, the Popular Democratic Party has won eight of the eleven elections and the two status plebiscites. This record of success at the polls gives the Popular Democrats confidence that Puerto Rico will remain a Commonwealth at least for the immediate future.

Many of the leaders of the Popular Democratic Party, however, believe that statehood will come about ultimately. In their estimation, however, the time is not yet right. Another five or ten years would be a more realistic prospect. They point out that while the Puerto Rican economy has improved substantially, it is not yet ready for the revolutionary changes that statehood would bring about.

As a Commonwealth, Puerto Rico does not pay federal income taxes. Statehood, with the obligation to pay such taxes, would bring about serious problems for lower- and middle-class Puerto Ricans. Federal taxes would diminish the purchasing power of too many of the less fortunate.

The Puerto Rican business community also feels threatened by a too quick move to statehood. When representatives of trade associations appeared before the Senate committee, they warned that changing the present tax structure would bring dire consequences to the profits of both large and small enterprises. The trade associations also told the senators that they were prepared to spend millions of dollars to educate Puerto Rican citizens as to their best option—delaying statehood for a period of years.

☆ THE CASE FOR STATEHOOD ☆

Enthusiasm for statehood has gradually accelerated over the past two decades as three successive American presidents—Jimmy Carter, Ronald Reagan, and George Bush—have openly backed it. President Bush not only expressed favor but is also known to have spent time in Ponce in 1989 discussing the matter with Luis Ferré, the founder of the New Progressive Party, which has waged an unrelenting campaign for statehood.

The unequivocal statements of three presidents have given the statehood adherents powerful ammunition as they spread word of the benefits of statehood.

Proponents of statehood discount the Popular Democratic Party claims that statehood might bring economic paralysis to Puerto Rico. They say that confidence is the prime element for an increasing economy, and that Puerto Rico as a state would inspire greater confidence for business on the island. More corporations from the mainland and from other nations would be more likely to invest in the island.

Statehood proponents also discount the claim of the *independencitas* that Puerto Rico would lose its Spanish culture. They argue that in the almost one hundred years that Puerto Rico has been a territory of the United States, it has maintained its Spanish heritage and that Spanish is still the official language of the island.

They also remind doubters that Hawaii still retains its original culture. Hawaii, they say, has improved both economically and culturally since it became a state, and that there should be no reason why Puerto Rico couldn't enjoy the same fate.

☆ **83** ☆

Puerto Ricans are also being reminded that their status as a Commonwealth positions the island as little more than a colony of the United States. While they do have representatives in Washington, they do not have a vote even on matters concerning their own welfare. They are not allowed to vote for the U.S. president even though they can send delegates to the nominating conventions. Statehood would give them all these desirable civil rights, including two Puerto Ricans to serve as United States Senators and two, perhaps three, voices in the House of Representatives, as spokespersons to look out for Puerto Rico's best interests.

As far as the United States is concerned, Puerto Rico is an important possession. Its strategic location at the entrance to the Caribbean has positive value. Statehood might well be in the best interests of the United States.

Sometime before the end of the twentieth century, it is entirely possible that Puerto Rico will achieve statehood. Whether it is the fifty-first state may depend on how soon. Which path will the island of Puerto Rico take?

SOURCE NOTES

☆ **CHAPTER 2** ☆
**BORIQUEN BECOMES
PUERTO RICO**

1. Bartholome de las Casas, Bishop of Chiapa
(1474–1566) *Historia de las Indias.* Lewis
Hanke, *Mexico Fondo de Cultura Economica,*
1951 (3 vols.), San Juan Public Library.

☆ **CHAPTER 5** ☆
THE MUÑOZ ERA

1. Juan Jose Osuma, *A History of Education in
Puerto Rico,* 1949.
2. Ismael Rodriguez Bou, "Significant Factors in the
Development of Education in Puerto Rico." Included in his *Status of Puerto Rico* (1966) pre-

pared for the United States Puerto Rican Commission.
3. Osuma, op. cit.
4. Ibid.
5. Ibid.

☆ CHAPTER 6 ☆
THE YEARS AFTER MUÑOZ

1. *El Mundo* (San Juan newspaper) March 28, 1968.
2. *The New York Times*, March 27, 1968.

PRONUNCIATION
GUIDE

NOTE: It is estimated that at least 5 percent of the world's population speaks Spanish. However, one country's pronunciation of a word may vary slightly from another's. Even on the island of Puerto Rico, pronunciations may differ slightly from one area of the island to another. The pronunciations offered here are those used by the majority of the islanders.

Antilles	an-TEE-yes
Arawak	AH-rah-wok
Arecebo	ah-re-SEE-bo
Barbados	Bar-BAY-dos
batey	ba-TAY
Boriquen	bore-EE-ken
Caparra	kah-PAH-rah
Carib	KAH-rib
Cepeda, Orlando	Sa-PAY-da, Or-LAN-do
Clemente	klay-MEN-tay

Colón, Rafael	Co-LON, Ra-fa-YEL
Hernández	Her-NAN-des
Culebra	Koo-LAY-bra
El Morro	el-MOR-row
Ferré	fer-RAY
Giral, Ramon Power	Hee-RAL, RA-moan
	Pow-WEAR
Hispaniola	Iss-pan-YOH-la
Independencitas	In-de-pen-den-SEE-tahs
Luis	loo-EES
Marín	mah-REEN
Mayaguez	mah-yah-GWES
Muñoz	moon-YOS
Ponce de Leon	PON-say day lay-OHN
Rivera	Ray-VER-a
San Juan	San-WHAN
Sanchez Viella	SAHN-chez Vee-YAY-la
Taino	tah-EEN-oh
Tobago	Toe-BAH-go
Venezuela	Ven-nay-ZWAY-la
Vieques	Vee-KEZ

FOR FURTHER READING

Alliota, Jerry. *The Puerto Ricans.* (The Peoples of North America series) New York: Chelsea House, 1991.

Dietz, James. *Economic History of Puerto Rico: Institutional Change and Capital Development.* New York: William Morrow, 1986.

Hauptly, Dennis. *Puerto Rico: An Unfinished Story.* New York: Atheneum, 1990.

Lewis, Gordon K. *Puerto Rico: Freedom and Power in the Caribbean.* New York: Harper & Row, 1976.

Melendez, Edgardo. *Puerto Rico's Statehood Movement.* Westport, Connecticut: Greenwood Press, 1988.

Perl, Lila. *Puerto Rico: Island Between Two Worlds.* New York: William Morrow, 1979.

Thompson, Kathleen. *Puerto Rico: Portrait of America*. Milwaukee: Raintree Publishers, 1985.

Walsh, Catherine. *Pedagogy and the Struggle for Voice: Issues of Language, Power and Schooling for Puerto Ricans*. Westport, Connecticut: Greenwood Press, 1990.

INDEX

ABOUT THE
AUTHOR

David Abodaher was born in Streator, Illinois, the son of immigrants from Lebanon. At the age of five, his family moved to Michigan, where he received his early education in Detroit parochial schools. It was during his college years at the University of Detroit and Notre Dame that he began his writing career.

Mr. Abodaher's first earnings as a writer began when he was sixteen. After his college years, he turned to radio, working as a writer and producer-director of dramas, many of which were heard on network radio.

After serving in the U.S. Signal Corps during World War II, he returned to Detroit and entered the field of advertising. He began writing books in 1960. Since then, he has had seventeen books published, all but one for young people.

Mr. Abodaher has always been a history buff, and many of his books reflect that interest. His other main hobby is travel. He has visited not only all American states, Canada, and Mexico but also most European countries and all nations in the Middle East. This book on Puerto Rico was inspired by about six trips to that island during the past ten years.

David Abodaher now lives in Southfield, Michigan, a suburb of Detroit. He has one daughter, Lynda, and a grandson, Adam Henderson.